MY TWISTED LITTLE WORLD

INDIRA ROY MANDAL

INDIA • SINGAPORE • MALAYSIA

Notion Press Media Pvt Ltd

No. 50, Chettiyar Agaram Main Road,
Vanagaram, Chennai, Tamil Nadu – 600 095

First Published by Notion Press 2021
Copyright © Indira Roy Mandal 2021
All Rights Reserved.

ISBN 978-1-63904-555-6

DEDICATION

I would like to dedicate this book to my father who has had an everlasting impact on my personality, and has contributed to being what I am today. Your hard work and determination have inspired many to bring about changes in so many lives. Thank you, Baba, for your support and unrelenting faith in me. I remember and salute you for embracing life's challenges and continuing to have faith in your deeds.

CONTENTS

LOCKDOWN DIARIES

FOREWORD

Prof. Tamal Kanti Ghosh
M.D., Ph.D (Med) MBA (Hospital Management)
Special Secretary (Medical Education)
Department of Health & Family Welfare
Government of West Bengal

Swasthya Bhawan
GN-29, Sector - V, Salt Lake City
Kolkata - 700091
Phone No. : 033 2337 4348
033 2333 0278
Email : mert.wb@gmail.com

FOREWORD

This book embraces the challenges that we face along with our children knowingly or unknowingly while being parents, mentors and caregivers. We cannot shy away from them but we need to address them in order to make the journey of life a bit more comfortable for the young ones as well as for us.

Mental health is a huge challenge when it comes to accepting and dealing with it. The challenge is compounded when one has to live and suffer silently with these problems as acceptance and stigma looms large on families affected by it. Recognizing and address in mental health issues by early intervention can go a long way in ensuring the child's progress..Hence it is important to consult a person who can guide and provide the inputs beneficial for the child and family.

Being in the Department of Health, Government of West Bengal,India, I have seen situations wherein we have had the worst times especially in the current scenario in terms of COVID 19 pandemic. Mental health is compromised due to various reasons during these times. Joining hands and helping our affected children can bring some normalcy in their stressed lives.

Prof. (Dr.)Tamal Kanti Ghosh 24|04|2021

Special Secretary (Medical Education)

Dept. of Health and Family Welfare,

Government of West Bengal,

PREFACE

For parents teachers and educators, who are an integral part of the child's life, and who are influential in nurturing the young minds and filling their 'tabula rasa' with confidence and love for themselves and their environment. In this world of competition, the need to achieve, the intent to be famous we forget that all of us including our children have the right to feel sad, angry, disturbed, ashamed, guilty, irritated, anxious, and depressed. The most important thing is to acknowledge these emotions as we acknowledge being happy, excited, motivated and confident. Working on these is difficult and helping someone to work on these is a bigger challenge. Can we simply share these uneasy feelings with our near and dear ones?

This is an attempt to celebrate each child, the uniqueness they are born with and the wealth of love and empathy they have in them. We just need to tap their potential, and create a better place for them. This is also a tribute to children and their parents suffering silently with certain disorders/handicaps and urging them to accept these challenges however difficult it may be so that others may follow suit and face the world with equal elan. Each of us has the right to live with our shortcomings and enjoy the hues life has to offer.

The mental health of children is severely impacted during lockdown. This is an attempt is to help our children withstand these tough times, help them understand the ramifications of the present conditions and instil in them a sense of hope to make the best of the current situation.

In the hope that we nurture a better tomorrow, we need to believe in the present.

ACKNOWLEDGEMENTS

I would like to thank Mrs. Sonali Sen, the Principal of Delhi Public School, Newtown and the teachers and staff of the school, who provided me with the exposure and guided me through the journey of understanding young minds. I am also grateful to the teachers and staff of Kendriya Vidyalaya, Ballygunge, Kolkata as well as 'The Calcutta Emmanuel School' for having introduced me to the fascinating and curious world of children and their nuances.

I would also like to thank my parents, my father for being my inspiration and my mother for selflessly caring for me, my brother and sister-in-law, my father-in-law for encouraging me, my husband Dr Palash Mandal for having given me the courage and the strength to achieve my goals. All of them have been a backbone in all my endeavours to deliver something novel and interesting. I would also take this opportunity to thank some of my friends who supported me throughout this venture. This book is a tribute to all the parents, caregivers, educators and society at large which is responsible for shaping young minds.

I am also indebted to the organisation 'Samikshani', which has provided me with valuable inputs during my association with them, enhancing my exposure and understanding of mental health and providing me with certain diagnostic skills required to deal with children.

Last but not the least my own son Soham has taught me a life changing lesson on parenting. I am grateful for all the experiences I have had so far, bitter or sweet, as they have helped me understand and appreciate people for what they are.

GOLDEN GIRL

When the adolescent girl of barely fourteen went out with her peers on a movie outing followed by lunch, she did enjoy the presence of her 'friends' liked the movie and lunch but somewhere deep inside felt out of the place. She had always wanted to go out with her friends have a relaxing time like every one of her age usually would dream of. Even in the company of her desired friends she felt lonely, uncared for, empty but put on a smile to show that everything was fine. Shamane, never really felt it would not be that exciting for her, as she had told her parents about the outing and they let her grudgingly go. An introvert, battling obesity and other health issues like polycystic ovarian disease, she was not the kind her peers would like to interact with, but they did not mind her presence as she was noninterfering and hardly put forward her opinions. She always wanted to say a few things and share her views, but something would stop her. Gradually she learnt to keep quiet. For the outing she had worn a dress that she had very carefully selected and had bought for her birthday last month and it was her parents' gift to her. She looked nice and refreshingly cool on that summer afternoon. She wanted to look like Nina and Rikkie, her friends, as she thought they looked extremely charming. Whilst they were having their lunch at a local restaurant, after enjoying the movie she sensed that some of them were talking about her and did even overhear a few comments pertaining to how she looked. Shamane tried to ignore her friends and thought it was her fault that she was overweight and that was the reason people talked about her. Instead of enjoying her lunch she just nibbled at some food. The boys in the group also gave more attention to Rikkie and Nina.

The outing ended with the friends dispersing for home from the restaurant, and Shamane had asked her dad to pick her up as she stayed further down the road. She went home and her parents checked on her as to how she had enjoyed the long-awaited outing to which she just smiled. She closed the door and sat quietly asking herself whether she enjoyed herself. She did enjoy the outing but wished she had enjoyed it even more. Leena another girl in the group would often see her quiet and reach out to her, but she did not go this time which made the discomfort pronounced. Nonetheless she continued with her routine throughout the evening trying to figure out what made her so 'different' from her friends and what could she do to be 'one of them'. As the evening rolled into the night, she ate her dinner quietly with her parents avoiding their questions, as she did not feel like answering them and then went to sleep.

Raina and Shabir, Shamane's parents had been concerned about their daughter's behaviour ever since she had attained puberty. A reticent child she hated herself, moreover her body. They even consulted different doctors for her physical condition but without any result. Shamane did talk about her unhappiness regarding the way she looked and that it marred her confidence. Her parents did try and explain that there was no problem with that, but that did not convince her. She kept all her questions, unacceptance by her peers, feeling bad about the way she looked, to herself, and most of all stopped loving herself. She nurtured the belief that she was not worth being accepted! Her only hope was Leena who understood her, but she was careful not to overwhelm her with her problems lest she lost someone who accepted her the way she was.

Next day in school she met Leena and spoke briefly about the outing but did not talk too much about her feelings, but Leena knowing Shamane, she just held her hand. Leena was one of the very few to be by her side and one of the reasons why she wanted to go to school. She felt that warmth and comfort in her company which she did not find anywhere.

Lenna went to Shamene's house the next day and asked her parents if she could join dance classes with her, to which they agreed. Shamane was a good dancer but due to her lack of confidence she had dropped out, which left a void in her. She resisted initially but gave in to Leena and they started enjoying their classes together. It took some time for Shamane to get back to her dance routine, but she regained her confidence and even stated knocking off those extra pounds. Soon it was the 'Annual Day' in school and Shamane was in the dance troupe which was to perform on that big day. She was nervous, though she had rehearsed and held Leena tightly till the performance began. She performed well, bringing tears to her parents' eyes and the applause from the audience left her shaking and she felt as if it was a fairy tale. The journey began from here and there was no looking back for her. She participated in many programmes and loved what she did. She was at peace with herself, happy and content and most importantly, brimming with confidence.

Technically Shamane suffered from **body dysmorphic disorder**. She was body shamed not always overtly, but covertly and the perception that her friends and the world projected about certain body types were certainly not correct though 'desirable'. It taught her that she was ugly, unwanted and not fit enough to be around with other girls and boys who had the desired body type. Now the question lies in 'desired by who?'. In her desire to be like her friends she hated herself, forgot happiness and dwelled in self-pity. This attribute would not have bothered her if she was a resilient and a no-nonsense type of personality. She took things to heart, therefore comments, statements even gestures left an indelible mark on her psyche. This haunted her, but she kept up her efforts to be one among her 'friends'.

Supporting this kind of an adolescent child, making her feel it is fine not to be accepted or liked by all, and even having one friend, who understands you, is important. This may be a challenging task but not an impossible one and the only thing it needs is reaffirmation that it is fine to be as you are, we are with you, letting the child pursue her interests so as to get the much-awaited appreciation, communication with people who are accepting, channelizing his/her time in something that would not allow the negative thoughts to creep in. In short, one has to accept himself/herself in order to be able to be confident. That acceptance and love for self goes a long way in determining the relationship with others. Parents, teachers, elders, peers all play a pivotal role in shaping a confidant personality irrespective of however you look and whatever you are.

SMITTEN

Tanya, the second born of her parents was a very obedient and studious child. Her parents were very proud of her and gave her all that she needed to excel in her studies as well as other spheres. They were also somewhat strict in their upbringing thinking that that was very important for her all round development. Her brother on the other hand was not dealt with so strictly, but she never complained as she got the love and affection from all of them. Tanya was in the final grade in school and all her teachers and family members had hopes pinned on her career and academics.

Silently, Tanya admired Sandip, a boy in her class, since her eighth grade and the journey of friendship started. They occasionally went out with common friends. This friendship nurtured into a bond which they called 'love', and thus came times when they talked to each other over the phone very often, sat next to each other in school and shared their tiffin. They were living the life which they wanted and enjoyed each other's company a lot.

One day Tanya's mother was summoned to school, and she was nervous as she thought that Tanya must have fallen ill. She hurriedly went to school and found to her utter disdain that an angry coordinator of the class asked her to wait as she had been called by the Principal. The crying girl sat on a chair and her mother started comforting her, and on the opposite side sat Sandip and his parents with fear written on their faces. Tanya's mother knew Sandip and his parents as her daughter's friend and they had met before. Soon she was asked to enter the Principal's room and she narrated something which shook up the frail lady and she sat shell shocked looking at the Principal, Vice Principal and others in the room in sheer disbelief. The Principal told her that Tanya and Sandip had kissed in school and they were seen by their friends and this was reported to the teachers. Tanya's mother had nothing to say when she was told that she was being suspended from school for some time, and she left. She was also told that she would be called later for a written intimation on what had transpired.

Both left school, Tanya crying inconsolably as she never thought that a girl of her kind would ever be punished so harshly. Her mother did not speak a word, her face pale and hung with shame and both reached home. The incident was narrated to her father who took it on himself to support his daughter at this point and his wife too because she had faced the entire wrath of the school authorities. He was an extremely level-headed man with immense patience and could handle situations like this very well. Though he too was pained, keeping his emotions aside he thought that his daughter needed him the most now.

After an exceptionally quiet dinner where all ate frugally, Tanya's father came up to her and asked her about the what had happened. She was close to him and she did confess that they both liked each other and did not realize when she got carried away emotionally and kissed each other. She also said it was a grave mistake but pleaded with her father that she should not be given such punishment by the school and she would never repeat such actions in the future. Her father held her tight and hugged her and told her that it was praiseworthy that she realized her mistake and would approach the school authorities for relaxation in the punishment that was meted out. He also told her that since this was a mistake, she should accept some kind of punishment from the school as the school functioned according to some rules and regulations.

After a week Tanya's father met the Principal and the other school authorities and begged forgiveness and even agreed to give in writing that if she indulged in any such act in the future, the school could take any decision, in turn he asked them to revoke the long-term suspension and lessen the number of days. The school not relenting to him, asked him to sign a letter stating a period of one and a half month's suspension, and he had to sign it.

In the meanwhile, though dejected, Tanya's father helped Tanya come out of her guilt and took her to play golf and went shopping with her and even bought her a pet dog who gave her enough company and loved her to the moon. Slowly and surely, Tanya was trudging back to normalcy and her father told her 'Tanya, do not blame anyone for your action. You have got the time to think reflect and plan, therefore make use of this time. You are such a bright child; you need to show the school that you can make them proud. In what way you may surge ahead is your call, but dear go ahead and make all of us proud, my princess.'

The Board Exams approached and Tanya had studied really hard for it as she was determined to make her parents very proud of her and wipe off all that they had been through because of her. It was a big day as the whole family sat in front of the computer and waited with baited breath and of course Tanya had topped her school in the exams and tears rolled down her eyes as she held her father tightly and said 'Thank you Papa for being with me'. Her mother and brother hugged her and shouted out in joy.

Tanya's parents were summoned again by the school this time' but this time they went with confidence, pride and with their head held high as they saw their princess receive a prestigious award from the school as well as a coveted scholarship to continue her academics.

Very often we bring our insecurities, biases, and lack of empathy when we deal with such issues. *We suffer from several idiosyncrasies which lead to education on sex and sexuality being a taboo. Children never have a clear or the right approach to the subject and often have certain sketchy information downloaded from the internet or rely on their equally inexperienced peers on the issue to bombard them with half-baked information and satiate their curiosity.*

More importantly, they are never comfortably or normally speaking about their bodies as they should be at their age and often end up getting rebuked by parents, teachers and so-called family members if they express their desire to know about it. Failing to understand that curiosity is natural, these topics should be dealt with as easily as other subjects. This will give them a chance to express their feelings, be correctly informed and even make better choices as far as sex and sexuality is concerned. It may not solve a whole gamut of problems relating to the issue but can prevent a lot of instances like Tanya's and to allow her friendship to mature into a long lasting and healthy relationship, and who said 'love' cannot be healthy.

A teenager is at a stage of exploration, whether it is friends, new devices, clothes, new ideas and innovation of all sorts, mind is both baffled as well as creative at this age, and all that it requires is the impetus to move in a direction with a goal in mind. Hand holding, explaining, and listening to them to show someone cares is very important at this stage. Tanya could have gone into severe depression had she not been supported by her father and had she not been that resilient, but we must remember that everyone is not the same and all children like Tanya do not have a happy end to their story. Some cannot bear the consequences, and their fragile mental state may lead them to a point of no return, therefore a comforting presence and a non-judgemental attitude could encourage communication from their side leading to a healthy dialogue.

'Punishments' rather than 'rectification' does not address the root cause nor does it 'eradicate' any behaviour. They are adolescent children and they need to be dealt with sensitively in order to bring about any change. By punishing we encourage rebellion and anger and at the end we are not achieving our goal of addressing the root cause of the problem.

In Tanya's case, the long-term benefit of the child should be kept in mind. Regular counselling of such children and sessions on family life education should be imparted to all adolescents. A friend/confidant could help her along with a teacher who could guide and monitor her in school. It is not only the duty of her parents to help her, but the collective responsibility of society to ensure that she is responsible for her actions.

A child's life could change either for the better or for the worse depending on coping mechanisms in a crisis and the support that they get in that situation. Our endeavour should be helping the child to focus on the future and look at the past as a lesson learnt.

CRUSHED

Roshan is in the 12th grade and he was on the last leg of finishing school. Being a meticulous child and an achiever in co-curricular activities he was quite a popular student in school. Teachers as well as students loved to listen to his poetic skills and often, he emerged victorious in many competitions. Being philanthropic and kind-hearted he helped whoever needed his assistance and this gave him immense satisfaction which others could never fathom. All seemed to be going well when one fine day he expressed the desire to enact a street play for the awareness of the LGBT (lesbian and gay bisexual and transgender) communities. As he was leaving home for a long time and taking part in a deviant activity, he did take permission from his parents, but they were very uncomfortable with the entire event.

The event went off well so did Roshan's act. He was praised for his writing and acting skills and his joy knew no bounds. He had achieved many accolades in his student life but this was very special for him, as he felt that for the first time he contributed in his own way to this small community. His happiness knew no bounds, and he rushed home to share the news with his parents. To his disdain, as he spoke to them, they had nothing much to say and they just murmured 'good', and went off to bed. Roshan was a little surprised to get such a lukewarm response from his parents and went to sleep.

Days kept passing by and the appreciation made Roshan contribute even more to the cause of the community and he even made several friends. Roshan's parents came to know about his intense feelings for the LGBT community and his several friends from amongst them, and they were visibly upset and wanted to talk to him. This talk was more of non-acceptance of Roshan's friendship with the transgender community by his parents as this would endanger their position in society as well as amongst their relatives. After hearing his parents Roshan firmly told them that he would continue to do this and he could not be stopped, and the conversation did not have a pleasant end. None of them willing to relent or understand the other, it just resulted in nothing but cacophony without serving any purpose.

After a week Roshan's mother got a call from his friend's mother asking her inquisitively...... 'Has your son turned into a homosexual?'. She was so shocked that she could not reply and just kept quiet and eventually disconnected the phone. She was also livid with rage at her son and felt that her son had now let her down and she would have to hide her face in shame because of him. She waited for him to return so that she could ask him. After a hectic day at school and other activities that Roshan loved, he returned home to answer his mother's questions. With a blank expression he accepted that his sexual orientation was different and that he had come to know about it much later. Devastated and holding her head in between her hands, she did not know what to tell him and kept on nodding her head from side to side in negation. She left the room and she broke the news to his father when he returned home. His father sat on the sofa quietly and told Roshan that he was too young to understand all this and probably he was being misled. He even offered to take him to a psychiatrist. This night was the coldest and the loneliest night Roshan could think of in his life, and he vehemently kept reiterating that his sexuality had nothing to do with his mental health and it was his preference and not a result of mixing with anyone.

The next day he was dragged to a psychiatrist and it wasn't a pleasant experience for Roshan. He continued to attend school, but his friends too started behaving weirdly with him, and some of them even started avoiding him. His favourite teachers often looked at him with raised eyebrows and this started playing in his mind. He could not take this neglect and indifference from his parents as well as his friends. Now the only friends that understood him or he could speak to were from the LGBT group with whom he could identify. He felt comfortable in their company. Returning home became a torture, going to school was no more pleasurable and academics took a backseat. Roshan went deeper and deeper into the burrow and no one not even his parents extended a hand to help him come out. He certainly was not in the right frame of mind and all that he needed was some acceptance and understanding and he craved for it from his parents, but unfortunately, they thought otherwise.

The next day Roshan was nowhere to be found and his parents searched for him in every possible place they could but it was of no avail. They repented their behaviour, they badly wanted to have him back in the house and even lodged a complaint with the police. After two weeks they got the information from the police that he was sharing a room with the transgender community on the outskirts of the city. His parents went to meet him and begged him to return home as he would not be able to sustain himself because he was still a student. He informed them that he had taken a part time job and he would look after himself. They pleaded further so that he came home before the exams, but their plea fell on deaf ears. They even promised to accept him the way he was but Roshan's belief was shaken and he was torn to bits and he decided never to return home, that was now not home for him anymore. He looked at his parents and said in a calm voice...'if only you had asked me how I felt and how much I needed you. If only knew what I was going through.'

We are not born with firm beliefs and opinions; they are nurtured in us over time. ***Having a different sexual preference is not wrong, is not a crime, it is a choice, like what we choose to wear. They day we understand this, we can save several lives living and dying of guilt and shame.*** We talk about untouchability, the Dalits, the minorities but we conveniently fail to include the LGBT community in the discussion. Are there any benefits for them in terms of acquiring jobs, providing them with education and the like? Our society is not even educated enough to understand the difference between the transgender, transsexual et al and choose to call all of them as eunuchs or 'hijras'. *This marginalized community has learnt to live with ostracization, mockery, contempt, and come under a common umbrella for the masses, left to beg and dance at weddings and go and ask for money at a house where there is a new-born. Last but not the least, they are the most susceptible to sexual offences by so called 'normal' people. To top it all, if I may say, they are the most creative people with a lot of passion, sensitivity and excel in fields such as fine arts, filmmaking and performing arts.*

Freedom we have achieved, but we have a long way to go where liberation of our thoughts is concerned. It is so difficult for us to come out of our cocoons and embrace a different world and be happy. The notion of normalcy should change, and this change should be of our mindset and be a permanent one.

LIVEWIRE

Adi a child of grade 2 was shifted to a new school recently as his teachers in the previous school had lots of complaints about his behaviour, and this forced his parents to find a new school for him. In the new school, Adi was known as a happy child, but a child who would not sit on his seat for more than a few seconds. Complaints slowly started pouring in from all quarters about his restlessness and his conduct. Days seemed years to his parents and they tried to understand why their child was behaving the way he was, and what could be a possible solution to this. Each day Adi went to school, Maya, his mother would wait with baited breath for him to return without hurting himself or someone else. Adi's academics took a backseat and the whole focus was on controlling or rather changing his behaviour. He squirmed in his seat and was up and about in seconds. Adi threw everything he could lay his hands on, had very little appetite and sleep. He sometimes went round like a merry go round until his head started spinning and fell with exhaustion. This got elevated when Adi tried to kill a puppy in his locality and his mother fortunately stopped him. His parents consulted his paediatrician and he casually informed Maya and Umesh that it was his age which made him behave the way he did, and would be fine in a couple of years or as he grew up. There were other inputs reinforcing this problem which was that 'Adi is very naughty and needs to be disciplined'. Adi's parents were slightly unnerved because they had tried some disciplining techniques too including hitting their child. Adi somehow managed a year in his new school and the parents heaved a sigh of relief as he went to the next grade. Things became worse in the next year with Adi being sent off for tuition classes, as Umesh and Maya thought they would get some relief. To their dismay, the situation became grave and the child started resenting the regimented schedule even more and his behaviour went downhill.

Just when things were looking very grim for Umesh and Maya and they had surrendered to their fate thinking that formal education was almost impossible for Adi, a friend of Maya, on hearing about Adi very patiently, referred her to a specialist for such children. Initially she was apprehensive and even denied that Adi did not need any specialist's advice, treatment or therapy. On discussing with her husband, they thought that they could give it a try as there was nothing to lose.

On a Saturday morning after a prior appointment, they visited Shruti the clinical psychologist in her chamber along with Adi. Shruti heard Umesh and Maya and observed Adi and familiarized the parents with a clinical condition called **ADHD or Attention Deficit Hyperactive Disorder.** She came to a conclusion after seeing the symptoms and interacting with the parents and child and after conducting a test for the child. This was a condition which needed immediate attention and intervention. After knowing about the symptoms of the disorder, Maya and Umesh tried to understand the condition or disorder. They were also referred to the psychiatrist as they were told by the psychologist that a doctor could confirm whether he required medication. Both of them resented the idea but they did accept the condition. They even searched for online remedies. They took Adi for some sessions but they did not seem to work very well. He continued to be very agitated, irritated and roamed about the house like a motor and in school the therapies did not show too much of a difference as he was still hitting other children and throwing things. This is when Maya and Uday gave in and visited the psychiatrist and appraised him of Adi's condition. He listened but explained to them that for some time Adi would need some medication as this was a disorder which had physiological bearing. He also informed them that being educated parents they should treat this condition like any other problem of the body and never ignore it. He also advised them to continue with therapy and have patience.

It has been three months that Adi has been continuing with his therapy and medicines. He does feel drowsy at times as a side effect of the medication but he is much more manageable than before and continues to attend school for a certain amount of time and is helped at home for his academics and other co-curricular activities by a special teacher. He is not completely cured of his condition but has started the journey to make a headway towards progress in life.

ADHD or Attention Deficit Hyperactive Disorder is a condition where a child can never be seated for even a few seconds, and behaves like a spring wound in action. To a layman it may just seem that a child is naughty but on careful observation it can be seen that he/she refuses to listen, hear, speak and is driven by any kind of stimuli. ***These children usually have very little appetite and sleep, they hurt themselves and others, refuse to listen to authority, love any kind of external stimulation, and if left untreated, they tend to have problems with law and order.*** They may indulge in violence may hit/kill animals too. ***They also suffer from anxiety which is often deep rooted and may not be outwardly manifested.*** More than the clinical facts stated, one must understand that no strange behaviour must go unnoticed in children. The parents are very vital in providing inputs as far as their child's behaviour is concerned as well as in instilling in some behaviour in children. We must also remember that every hyperactive child is not a child with ADHD. Let the specialists do their work and the parents observe and note the behaviour. However certain things we need to know are that sweets, fast food, junk food aggravate the condition. ***Therefore, stick to homemade food, and take out children to parks for at least one and a half hours of play daily, to let them 'release their energy'.*** Teach them things differently with activities and more of visual stimuli rather than plain pencil and paper. ***Lastly, understand that this is a problem with the 'wiring' of the brain, a physiological problem,*** which will slowly and surely get resolved, ***and may require medication,*** therefore address it, do not escape from it.

DANCING DEVILS

They say books are man's best friend. Well, are they? Not for all, and it was certainly not for bubbling Babli. Attempts to make her learn and write all went in vain. All that they would get a couple of hours after coaxing, explaining and shouting was some kind of modern art on a piece of paper. No matter how many hours of explanation were put in, the result ended up being the same. 'Dim witted', disinterested, not able to cope with academics were some of the explanations put forward to describe her. Babli, however, had a special knack in solving puzzles. She was quick as lightening and as adept as a professional when it came to construction with the *'Lego'*, or *'mechanics'*, to produce something as stunning as a monument or object. Her parents couldn't seem to fill in the blanks with regards to academics, her poor performance in school and the masterpieces she had created at home with the help of blocks. Was she really dull, below average and would she make it to the next grade in school? For all these years Babli's mother took up the responsibility of academics and made sincere attempts to teach her but the results were not very encouraging. She excelled in spatial recognition and was keenly interested in the logical section and the puzzle section of books. She was loved by her fine arts teacher and her Maths teacher (because of her innate ability in Geometrical constructions) and would participate in almost all the competitive programs related to fine arts. Days passed by and Babli would spend most of her time making 3D objects with paper or cardboard boxes and even created lovely objects out of mashed paper. Her mother used the rest of the time trying to grow her interest in academics.

Babli's academics continued to suffer and it was beyond her mother's comprehension as to how to tackle the situation. She expressed her concern to her relatives and friends and all of them had different suggestions and views which confused her even more. She knew her child and was not willing to accept that she was a child with low intellect knowing what she could do. She started changing her way of instructing her. She used cards, colours, boards, sand, colour paper and even took her on small outings to show her or make her experience what she had been taught in school. The changed the mode of instruction and made it appealing, interesting and something that made more sense to her daughter than just alphabets, numbers displayed in front of her. Unburdened with the weight of these digits and letters, she actually understood and learnt. She learnt how to 'create' the letters and then words and not just memorize them. It was a struggle for Babli and her mother, but they did continue their struggle for a few years. She barely managed to pass in the 'examinations' in school initially but later on performed better. Her aim was never to pursue the academics just to obtain a degree. Babli was always made for the creative world. She managed finish school and took up architecture as one of her subjects. Her mother helped and supported her in all ways and encouraged her to walk on the path she chose.

She completed her higher education in architecture and opened her own creative arts company with a lot of passion and hard work, her mother by her side, and today she is the owner of a renowned architectural company.

Learning disability or Dyslexia is a term for inability to spell write or comprehend a particular language. It is an umbrella used to encompass other disorders in learning like **dyscalculia (difficulty with digits), dyspraxia (immaturity in organization of movement in relation to writing as well as walking speaking etc) and dysgraphia (problems with spelling and handwriting).** They may not be identified by many and may be passed off as the child being naughty and disinterested. This story of

Babli tells us about her learning disability which hampers her academics but with her mother's support is able to get over it. Babli's mother is not aware of the technical term of her daughter's problem but manages to help her sail through it. ***Ignorance is not bliss in such cases.*** The first thing about dyslexia or any leaning disability is that the people with dyslexia are intelligent which means that they have above average intelligence. This is confirmed by the fact that Babli was good in fine arts, loved construction with blocks and excelled in Geometry. ***Her logical thinking was not impaired.***

Learning disability should not be seen as a disability, but the ability to do something differently. History resonates the fact that people with dyslexia have often been creators and inventors and have given the world that we could never dream of. When a child gives us cues, is a little different from other children, we should go ahead with these signals as miracles can happen if we understand and help the child conquer these difficulties.

MISSING THE EYE

There is nothing more than that which meets the eye. Well, there is! Everyone is different and has come with his/her set of perfections and imperfections. We often try to classify people either negatively or positively. Have we ever thought that there is a reason as to why someone is labelled that way? Here comes the nature Vs nurture theory. Some children have an innate way of behaving the way they do and others react to the environment around them. This is yet another simple and interesting story of Sam.

Sam could not express himself since the age of two years when other children overtly expressed their feelings in words or actions. His parents were not aware of the fact that his behaviour was different from other children. It was at the age of two years that Miranda and Joe, Sam's parents began to feel all was not well with their son. He could not speak like the others, never saw anyone in the eye when they talked and made a strange humming sound all the time. He was fascinated by just one toy of his, a red car, though he had many, and would make it go round and round in circles whenever he had it. He however enjoyed music and would sit still when music played and would nod from side to side humming the tune beautifully and in sync. His parents would often wonder that Sam who would not be able to pick up things like other children, would however hum the tune of songs perfectly. What was the matter? They were upset with the fact that mainstream schools refused admission to Sam. They had no idea as to where to go and what to do. Sam grew older and his problems worsened. He could not get admission to any formal school even at the age of five. The panic continued for Miranda and Joe who were too scared to articulate their problems to their friends and relatives. They suffered in silence. They thought it was the end of the road as far as Sam was concerned. Then by chance, Miranda and Joe met another family with a child behaving like Sam at shopping complex nearby and finally mustered the courage to go and ask them about their child and talk about Sam. Initially the family was expressed apprehension, but then, slowly started speaking about their child. The child was a pretty girl a little older than Sam and was muttering to herself and constantly swinging her arms. Sam also tried to observe the girl and they did communicate with each other but rather differently. They touched each other and then swung their arms wildly. Sam made certain sounds and tried to express his happiness which his parents understood. He was communicating after a very long time with an 'outsider', as his parents seldom brought him out. When he started making loud sounds, his parents hushed him up in embarrassment. The girl however, did not make sounds but uttered certain words clearly like her name and addressed

Sam as a 'boy'. Sam's parents had an informative conversation with the girl's parents over a cup of coffee and took details about the school the girl was going to and the progress made by her.

This was the first time Joe and Miranda saw a ray of hope in the dark. They immediately contacted the school, which was a special school and to their surprise, he got admission there and they were also appraised of his condition. Sam made progress, but very slowly, and his parents were told that this disorder would be there for life. The school would however take on the task of training and educating him to the extent that was possible. Since they were told about Sam's interest in music, special classes were arranged for him and he seemed to enjoy music the most. He started singing instead of just humming and when he was in his teens even released a music album of his own.

Miranda and Joe found immense solace in the fact that Sam had achieved a lot keeping in mind the hurdles faced and thanked God for having met a family who had helped them to address Sam's issues.

The condition mentioned in the abovementioned story denotes autism, and this falls under the **Autism Spectrum Disorder or ASD**. Sam was a moderately autistic child with inability to express himself which is the main symptom of ASD. Sam's **speech is still not clear** which is another characteristic of an autistic child. Another significant symptom is that **there is no eye contact.** Often, by the age of two years the caregivers do understand that the child's responses, way of interacting with the environment and activities are different. **This lasts as long as the person lives. People not understanding them often call them weird, violent, ill behaved, rude and loud. We must understand that these are the coping mechanisms of autistic children who cannot express themselves in any other way and have a serious social interaction problem.** Special schools for such children may provide handholding which is important for these children, though they can be enrolled in mainstream schools. Too much of stimulation, for example loud sound and disruption in routine often upsets an autistic child. Therefore, when taking care of them, these must be taken into consideration. They also possess 'islands' of talent, which in Sam's case was singing. These talents should be tapped enabling them to pursue it and vent out their feelings and emotions which are often trapped due to lack of expression which is characteristic in their case. Autism is not the end of the road, but a beginning of a difficult and different journey to view the world in a different light. Last but not the least, I would like to mention that some very famous people in the world have suffered from this disorder and yet conquered it to make a mark for themselves. Accept and help the autistic child.

TICK – TOCK

Manju had an adorable side to herself her selfless nature, and her smile just personified that aspect of her personality. She had a few very good friends and everything was fine except the one thing she was not able to control, which was her involuntary shaking of the head. The moment it happened she could feel losing control over herself and a feeling of helplessness crept in, and until it stopped, she would almost act like she was doing it at someone's behest. This was not understood nor taken well by all and the most common consequence would be that she would be mocked at and then be embarrassed about herself.

She had tried many a way to get over this, but wasn't successful. Her close friends were of great strength and they had accepted her the way she was and respected her intelligence and her heart-warming personality. She was average in academics and always dreamt of serving the poor. Manju helped her teachers, friends and parents at all times they needed her and she had carved a small cosy niche for herself in the big world, not aware that this world had many surprises in store for her. She found strength and solace in her small world and often felt that altruism is the best way to escape the 'handicap' she possessed. Manju did try and educate her classmates, friends relatives and teachers about her condition, and some did understand it, but most of them hardly cared as it did not have an impact on their lives, some were indifferent while others taunted her. She continued with these experiences only to complete school.

She entered an entirely different world of higher education, a college and of course everything was new to her and each day brought in surprises for her. She did make some friends but mostly faced ridicule, insult and shame. She felt she had got over school with a lot of difficulties and would not allow these obstacles to get in her way. There were days she could not talk to anyone and keeping her selfless nature in mind she did not want to trouble anyone with her worries. She wielded the weapon of self-respect with aplomb, and ignoring others who tried to demoralize her and soon very slowly found herself amongst another small circle of friends in the college. She was elected as the Secretary of the Social Welfare Society in college and did challenging work for a few orphanages. At home she would spend her time in writing about her experiences and telling her parents about her plans to open a non-profit organisation to help the underprivileged children. She never dreamed of something very 'big'. Manju dreamed of something very 'different' and knew that she would be able to achieve it. She emerged as one of the most creative and hardworking students in the college and there were a few teachers who had helped her throughout the journey. She may not have been acknowledged for it anytime formally, but her parents, teachers and some close friends always made her feel that she was a blessing to them.

It wasn't that Manju was never demoralized, dejected, shattered, and felt miserable, but each time she felt such emotions she would sit down quietly and think about the children that she had seen on the streets, the maid in her house who was going through such a challenging life and her new born cousin who had lost his mother when she was born. When she thought about all these, she thanked God for giving her a secure and a safe place to live in and lovely parents who were always by her side. The strength that she drew from thinking and thanking was enough fuel to sustain her for life.

Today Manju owns a non-profit organisation which works for street children, their education, safety, nutrition and other aspects of their development. She is very content doing what she always wanted to do and sits on her chair with her head uncontrollably nodding at times, but what she has under her control, is her life.

This disorder often called the 'Tourette's syndrome' poses as a social difficulty and though seemingly may not be a threatening one, it is indeed a debilitating one. It can cripple one socially, cause ostracization, depression and the like. Manju was one of the lucky girls to have found support in her family and few friends, but this may not always be the case. The rejection and humiliation can have serious ramifications and may cost the life if the person. The way out of this is ***awareness and education***, so that the society not only accepts people with Tourette's syndrome but also comes forward to help them so that this does not affect the self-esteem of the person in any way. Learn about this, help people to live with this and most importantly accept this.

SUBSTANTIAL

Ranjan a vibrant young boy who loved sports went for his daily practice after school. He loved his practice sessions and would return home tired after a long day but rejuvenated and ready for the next day. He was energy unlimited and ever since he started walking, he never sat still. He was a complete 'outdoor' person. The very thought of the playground, the streets, his playmates and a football or his cricket bat would serve as a catalyst for him to leave for play. There was an unexplained rush of adrenalin when he saw or thought about the playground. His weekends were mostly devoted to the outdoors, fields, streets wherever there was space to play.

His life revolved outdoors and he wanted to make a mark in the world of sports. Every time he polished his shoes or used an adhesive to mend innumerable things in his play kit, the smell would transport him to a different world. He just loved the smell of these substances. He would often take charge of polishing everyone's shoes in the house.

There were many more friends that Ranjan made when he played and as he grew up, and he was immersed in his own world. As his circle of friends grew bigger there were few of them who played not because they loved to play like Ranjan, but to pick out young boys and introduce them to vices which could destroy them. Ravi was one of them. Ravi was four years older to Ranjan who was fourteen and was an entrant in his life at a point when he could control him. Ravi observed Ranjan very closely since the time they met and even noted his fascination for the smell of certain substances. He would often ask Ranjan to bring his bag and open it for him and give him water. Most of the times Ranjan could smell adhesives and very strong ones in his bag and would playfully sniff it. This did not remain playful after a few weeks, as Ranjan himself started to find excuse to open Ravi's bag and would find quite a few substances that were 'so good to smell'. This became a habit very soon and Ravi having Ranjan in his grip very soon he graduated to other addictive substances. In a couple of months Ranjan was addicted to sleeping pills, cough syrup, glue and a few other substances.

His lively and charming personality was replaced by a manipulative and a selfish self who would also lie. He had become an addict at a young age and this took a toll on his parents as they were completely unaware about the whereabouts of their son and had always supported his physical well-being in terms of play. Little did they realize that this freedom given to their son would cost them this much! They contacted a doctor with the help of some of their friends and put him under treatment. This cost Ranjan two whole years and he had to spend these two years being carefully monitored and staying at the deaddiction centre for days together. There were hiccups here too as he relapsed a few times and went back to his addiction but now after five years Ranjan is recovering but the alluring and evil world of addiction will always beckon him. Needless to say, if he falls prey, he will go back to where it all began but if he looks ahead, he can battle these small evil pleasures for something big in life and that is, his dream of becoming a sportsman.

Addiction or substance abuse is a big challenge among the youth, which many youngsters confront. This mostly comes to light when the person exhibits certain symptoms like lying, insomnia, restlessness, no adherence to any schedule, decline in academic performance, relations with the wrong kind of people, discomfort with family and many more. To overcome this, awareness and exposure to the positive instances, simple joys and hardships to attain these joys, feeling of achievement on having accomplished a small milestone and proper guidance is necessary. *Education on substance abuse should be prioritized* and should not be a topic of taboo. On attaining a certain age father and son for example can talk about alcohol, its right way of consumption, quantity of consumption and may even choose to drink together. It is not a question of promoting alcohol for the gen next, but simply satiating their curiosity at home instead of having a sneak peek outside home for it. Chances are they will at least share with you about their friends, peers and others and some their activities outside home. *Sermonizing and being a control freak will only give the caregivers/parents satisfaction leaving the actual welfare of the child as less important.* Remember, we are dealing with children into adolescence and have to keep our feeling of being superior aside when dealing with them. *The best education and exposure one can give to a child is by giving them company and being available to them. They cherish and remember this forever.*

BY YOUR SIDE

Ishaan the seventh grader was simply the flamboyant boy one had ever seen. He used to attend school with a lot of fervour and zest but would hardly concentrate on his classes. He had a group of friends who would pay heed to his pompous nature and assist him in all his activities pertaining to his arrogance and building of his 'self-esteem'. He was rude to his teachers, passed statements loaded with innuendos at friends and never obeyed any rules. He often got punished but that made him more and more resilient and led him to doing what he wanted to do, defy others.

Ishaan came from a well to do family where his mother was an entrepreneur and his father was a Managing Director of a multinational company. They hardly had time for him and instead of giving him the time that they ought to, they compensated with gadgets electronic goods, throwing parties and even gave him cash in hand which was a lot for a twelve-year-old to handle. He bought things at his own will, went out to often with his friends to malls, often had his dinner outside, bought expensive gifts for his friends which wasn't a surprise for most of them.

Reading this, one may think that the fault is Ishaan or his parents for not spending enough time with him. The deterioration in his behaviour lay in the fact that instead of understanding the root cause of the problem, there were adults always trying to correct him. Ishaan was averse to being corrected and hated it if someone tried to sermonize. He just wouldn't take it. It was then that he made a new friend who had come from a different school. His name was Sandeep and he was a popular child because of his cheerful disposition and his vibrant nature. Ishaan was initially jealous of Sandeep because he was a crowd puller but Sandeep noticed Ishaan and the way he would communicate with others and his attitude which made him think that something was wrong with him. Sandeep approached Ishaan gently, and began talking to him about topics that interest boys of that age like sports, cars cinema and the latest gadgets in the market and many more. Sandeep slowly seemed to gain his confidence. One day, Ishaan got into serious trouble for bringing an expensive smartphone to school. Sandeep helped him handle the situation in a way in which he was not severely punished. Sandeep took the opportunity to talk to Ishaan at length that day by inviting him to his place. He asked him what was troubling him, and offered to help him as he considered him his close friend. This touched an emotional chord in Ishaan and he broke down in front of Sandeep.

It was clear to Sandeep that this boy actually had no one to tell him right from wrong, no one to scold him in his formative years and no one to hug him when he went back home. Everyone close to him apart from his so-called group of friends in school were busy. He poured his heart out to Sandeep and it was at this time that Sandeep realised that Ishaan had so many material things in his life but there was a vacuum where love, care, concern and bonding with his family was concerned. Ishaan's teachers and parents often put him off as a naughty child but beneath so many layers of naughtiness there was a child yearning for love attention and some patience, which he got from Sandeep. He made him realise how worthy and how valuable he was as he encouraged him to take part in all the school activities. Surprisingly, Ishaan did well and the other side of the boy came as a surprise to many. Slowly, Sandeep worked on his behaviour which would make him earn praise from his teachers and friends. He also motivated Ishaan to visit old age homes, orphanages to donate some of his pocket money and spend time with the less fortunate people there. All these activities and mainly Sandeep's influence changed Ishaan completely. He certainly became an important part of the class who would help in organizing preparing and participating in various awareness programs in his community and outside. His hidden empathy and humility were all that was needed to be tapped to allow him to explore and use them in his day-to-day life. Today both Sandeep and Ishaan are working as responsible staff for a leading organization working in the field of Health, and have achieved what they wanted to, giving society its due.

Ishaan was fortunate to have a friend in Sandeep, but we need many more of such children, parents and teachers or even extended family who could do the job which Sandeep so beautifully and effortlessly did. Behaviour is an outcome, so changing it needs a change in the mindset. If the feelings change so will the outcome. This does not happen only with children, but with adults also, who are often judged based on their external attributes. See reason for bringing about change so that it is a permanent one.

UPS AND DOWNS

The face and form, against the norm

As I wish to attend the prom.

There are questions to my loved ones,

Why does this child, by his friends, get shunned?

Looks different, does he?

Walks and talks way to awkward that's why must
be.

The eyelids droop and a small chin cannot hide

The flat wide face with a sweeping tide.

I continue to run, but just for fun

As I know I look clumsy and there's lots to learn.

I am slow but willing to finish, the lessons in life
taught to diminish

Thoughts of abstaining and that of curtailing,

My life and freedom, which I am unwilling.

I may not stand tall, nor have the same
intelligence

But my people have taught me to make a
difference,

by believing in myself and to live a life like a leaf
with dew.

Disappearing on the ageing of the day, but deep
inside glistens with rays on the array.

Down's syndrome is a genetic disorder. A child with Down's syndrome is educable and trainable up to a certain extent. They could either go to special schools where they have special trainers or could go to mainstream schools. Their life span could be somewhere from 50 to 60 years. This is not a curable condition, but certainly the earlier identified and intervened with the better the result.

People with Down's syndrome may have some or all of these physical characteristics: ***a small chin, slanted eyes, poor muscle tone, a flat nasal*** *bridge, and a protruding tongue due to a small mouth and relatively large tongue.*

Individuals with Down syndrome are at increased risk for obesity as they age. One may face a lot of challenges and dismal responses from people on training and dealing with children having this disorder, but the fact is that education and proper care improves their quality of life. They usually need a protected environment but that doesn't mean they remain homebound and ruminate within the confinement of a certain space. Agreed most pregnancies with the diagnosis are terminated, this does not mean that those who come into this world cannot be dealt with.

LOCKDOWN
DIARIES

THE NEW NORMAL

Yet another day,

I'm on my way...

Caught in the dreaded web

From which I can't get myself free

How is it that I am supposed to be?

No classes, but clanging of glasses

From the kitchen sink filled to the brink.

'Someone help me, I'm tired' a voice cracks

For there is no maid who was once hired.

Deserted streets, trees with shining peaks

Calling out, to fill them up ...

Amidst them lies a helpless pup.

Flouting all rules, undaunted by the virus

I shout out and call my friend Cyrus.

Together we go with food and water

Yes, the little one was someone's daughter.

Mommy dear who left her for food

Now beside her we gathered and stood!

ONLINE ONSLAUGHT

At morning eight, not the school gate,

But 'online classes' and 'Zoom' is the bait.

'Good morning' says the teacher,

But some can't reach her!

But alas to her surprise

Some are very wise...

They hide their face, as on the other side of the

dice...

Physics, Chemistry, Maths and History

All seem the same in the online mystery.

'All doubts clear, since exams are near?'

Teachers echo concern and fear.

'Online exams, what is the tension?

Try and understand it is like pension.'

Sounds rewarding, enticing too...

Once the Principal's gone, what to choose?

Laptop cacophony, desktop malware

Becomes the lifeline of our livewires.

WARRIOR

Doctor daddy goes for work,

Only to return when it is dark.

His clothes white and stark

All set to make a mark!

It is COVID ward and duty time

Wearing PPE, to me he looks sublime

Like an alien brought down to earth

Taken his time and all his worth.

Service continues all the way

Prayers, wishes all of them pay

Healing people and the world...

A painful chapter unfurls

Daddy, my hero, now lies in bed

He is COVID positive, that is all is said.

I can't touch him or kiss him goodnight

But from my room, I watch him alright.

Today may not be that bright

But for me, you are my 'shining knight'!

MY NEW TOY

My friends, my new phone,

I've entered a new zone.

It's the rush of a new hormone...

I've never sat with a laptop for so long

Whether it is Zoom, Netflix or a song.

WhatsApp is my best friend

On number ONE it does trend...

And to me great comfort it lends.

Mommy calls, calls again

On and on...goes the refrain

I choose to hear the bell of my phone

How proudly do this gadget I own!

Food ready is ready on the table...

'Me' fidgeting with the cable

'Addict' being my new label!

HOLDING HANDS

Opened my eyes, after brushing I see

Mommy in bed, still not had her tea.

She looks pale and very weak

'Please cook something', she sounded very bleak.

Never in my life I lit a flame,

But for trying I was game.

Searched the drawer found my favourite

Boiled water, made Maggie

And told her 'Bon Appetit'

I fed her slowly as she had fever

As she slowly ate, I could see her shiver.

'Mommy dear' I told her, 'it is fine'

'Tonight, with you and Daddy I shall dine.'

With some help I made some food

I felt good, as the test of time I withstood.

Three of us sat for dinner

After we ate mommy said,

'You are the winner.'

PEARLS OF WISDOM

Friendship is endearing, friends are caring,

Is it a cliché or just sharing?

Sounds simple, humble, nice words to mumble...

To carry it off, is like an ensemble

Well then, start with a jumble.

Empathy, selflessness, non-judgementality

Good to read in books of quality.

To practice more of these than preach

I must confess I did breach,

The love the confidence they had in me ...

And lo...where did I reach?

To myself, I was the best,

But all this was in zest.

My friends, my lifeline

They did outshine.

As for me, I fell in my own eyes

Never in my friends did I see despise!

OMNIPOTENT

Summing it up, lessons learnt
Sometimes got my hands badly burnt.
Nonetheless the calling of nature
Costed man to play the 'vulture'.

Abusing nature has been a bane,
Which has led to no gain.
Apart from the poor becoming poorer
Life becomes dreary and dearer.

Save nature, save lives, inculcate culture
Save brethren save the future!

Lessons learnt with arms folded,

'Lockdown' you got me moulded…

From 'me' 'myself' and 'mine'

Transformation to 'thee' and 'thine'.

CHILDREN AND THEIR WELL BEING DURING LOCKDOWN

Lockdown affects every stratum of the society and people continue to reel under the pressure of contracting the virus as well as stay healthy both physically and mentally even after the lockdown ends. Adults naturally have an innate coping mechanism for adjusting to this period, but children often get adversely affected as their confinement to their home is mostly triggers them on to increase their gadget time. With ***'nothing to do'*** as perceived by them it becomes necessity for their caregivers to focus on the productive aspect of these young creative minds as I believe that all children have something to give, to show, in their own way. Here is a list of probable activities that may help a child during this period of confinement:

- Since there are enough people at home to guide and take care of the child, they could be taught a lot of things during this time ***pertaining to life skills***. Start from the least difficult task and scale up. Basic things like putting your books toys in place should be started with. They can be asked to take out their old clothes books toys which are of no use and keep it in a place to donate it to an organisation. This is the first step to declutter and realize that one has more than he/she needs. This inculcates a sense of being sensitive to everyone around them.

- Ask the child to make a routine for herself/ himself with help if needed.

- Instead of focussing on the negatives of confinement try to make a list of things that the child can do which he/ she has never had the opportunity to do. Explain that this time would never come back and utilising this time for learning something unusual is going to be rewarding.

- Let the child ***know about the reason for confinement***. Let them know the basics about the disease and why they need to stay indoors. It is good to tell them that this confinement is going to last for some time, and they can learn new skills at this time. Having said this, it is not advisable to discuss in detail about the mortality and morbidity pertaining to the disease. No child would like to be overloaded with information so give as much information as required for the child.

- If the child misses the extended family allow him/her to interact on video calls skype or zoom. Have a time to enjoy old songs and movies and stories/movies with a message.

- Take the child out for a short walk taking the necessary precautions and before you take them talk to them about the hazards and the disease.

- Ask the child to pen down something on paper, write a short story etc. you never know how innovative their writing can be!

- Other creative activities like singing, dancing with the help of adults, playing **Antakshari** can be quite interesting. Use certain gadgets to enhance the activity.

- Ask the child what he/she would like to learn/do at this time. If they are confused it is the duty of the adult to place certain age appropriate as well as interesting choices in front of the child. For small children **no fire cooking, newspaper collage, cleaning their space, cleaning their toys, laying the table, helping in the garden** could be some of the options. Learning new skills like singing, sketching, amateur photography, how to take care of a pet and overall to be independent.

- This is an important period for the child to **teach him/her to be responsible.** Tell the child about the less fortunate people the value of food clothes and everything he/she has and which you probably haven't got the opportunity to talk about.

- Teenage children are a challenge to handle during normal times and lockdown makes them even more difficult to deal and reason with because of the thought processes that they are engaged in and the high energy reserve they have.

- Speak as a friend to the child letting him/her know that you are getting overwhelmed with all the household chores and you need help and **divide some work** amongst you and the child. In this way he/she respects you and shares your burden.

- It is a good time to have a heart-to-heart conversation with them and introduce them to **Family Life Education.**

- Give them some tasks like getting/ordering grocery etc. instead of using gadgets ask them to bring to light some skills they might be having and wanting to share with the world through the gadgets for example posting videos of some activities or for gadget freaks to develop something new (like a game).

- Teach/allow them to **cook a simple meal**.

- For children who are predominantly **'outdoor children'** and love physical activity is very stressful to stay indoors. It is advisable to encourage them to go to the terrace or use the open space in the front of the house to resume activities like walking exercising and playing in a limited way. They could also be encouraged to teach the other members in the family to play, exercise keep fit and rules of certain games. The child could be used as a teacher. He/she could be encouraged to talk to his play pals. The child could be asked to go outside to allow him/her to get a whiff of fresh air.

- Keep monitoring the gadget use of these children, allow interaction with friends and family but since they are at the mercy of the gadgets give them challenges during this time like wash their own clothes, cleaning their room, making the bed and making best out of waste.

- Reintroduce popular indoor games like **chess, Ludo, carrom or Chinese checkers** which are forgotten and unknown to most of today's children. Playing all these as a family helps bonding and is fun and then there is the bonus of becoming an expert at the game.

- Give them an **empty room** or space to themselves where they can play fight argue and prance around with their siblings or even alone.

- For teens especially it is important to **have them take care of senior citizens in** *the house*. They can do a good job at that provided adults trust them. There is a special bond between the grandparents and the grandchildren, and this helps strengthening the bond.

- Organize a house party for the children of the house to get rid of the boredom and give the children the burden of planning and executing it.

- Lastly do not forget that this time is the only quality time with your family therefore make use of it to know your children their likes, dislikes their worries and concerns at home, in school in the playground probably *some issues which you never thought of will surface and you can help them before it is too late and you go back to your busy routine life*. A new journey may begin for them if we use this time mindfully.

- Teach the child to be sensitive to the people like house helps, janitors security staff etc and others who work for us even during this period. In fact, it would be a good idea to imbibe in them the concept of dignity of labour.

- Let us not forget that children and adults who have never faced any mental health problems may actually face such problems during the pandemic. They may be affected directly or indirectly. If such situations occur, recognising the symptoms, taking professional help and supporting each other is of utmost importance. Situations like these are often major precipitating factors in mental illnesses thus reminding us repeatedly to take such concerns seriously. People confined to their homes for a long period of time makes the situation rather morbid.

- Most importantly teach them that *if someone needs help during this time of isolation, we should be ready to help with precautions as this pandemic can affect us too.* It is important to take care of oneself, but it is beautiful to take care of others as well.

- ***LET US TEACH OUR CHILDREN TO BE HUMAN AT THIS TIME OF CRISIS AND LET THEM KNOW THE IMPORTANCE SHARING AND CARING.***

FOR CHILDREN WITH MENTAL HEALTH CONCERNS

(GUIDELINES FOR THE LOCKDOWN)

- It is important that the parents stay in touch with the doctor/counsellor or the expert who looks after the child.

- *Please do not self-medicate your children or increase the dosage of medicine as per your convenience during this time* as **children with ADHD** can get bored and jittery during this time. They must be encouraged to do some physical activity on the terrace of their homes or within the boundary walls of their complex.

'**Zumba**' as a way of activity and exercise could be given a thought. Try to have them help you and keep them engaged fruitfully and follow a passion. Handling them is a major concern here not their behaviour. Understand the behaviour with patience and then respond, do not react or overreact.

- **Children with Learning Difficulty** could be given puzzles, or could be engaged in indoor games (which they are very good at), given reading material, engaged in storytelling or writing activities. Please ignore the spelling mistakes and play scrabble with them instead as a way of rectification.

- The biggest challenge is with children having **Autism or Asperger's disorder** as they have their routine of going to school, changed. This does not go well with them. They may not be able to express it but they will be upset. Create a classroom atmosphere at home with a temporary black board and ask the child to write on it. Keep a regulated tiffin time wherein the child along with you can have tiffin. At least some simulation of the school setting may be useful for him. Do not forget to give the child odd jobs. Usually, these children have a hidden talent. Now is the time to nurture it.

- **Children with conduct problems** need to be taken for short walks and be given some useful tasks. Even if they are playing let there be some innovation. Make them take the control, they love to be in control of things and it settles them. Very importantly exercise along with them regularly choose an application for it if necessary, on the laptop and run it while doing the exercise. It can be fun as well as engaging for everyone.

- *Lastly, please recognise that every child has a potential and this is the best time to nurture it. Do not underestimate the power of a young mind. Encourage them and the results will follow suit. Patience and perseverance always pay off. Love life, live life and stay safe.*

Whether it is lockdown time or not, the importance of intra personal and inter personal communication can be stressed upon for the well-being of the self. What keeps us going through these long periods of confinement or isolation is hope and dialogue with ourselves as well as with others. It teaches us to appreciate life, our care givers, our near and dear ones, our friends, our helpers and above all our own selves! We discover, reinvent and take a hard look at what magic we can do. Helping, sharing, expressing concern and being kind will heal the world. When it becomes a way of life, people will respect each other, indulge in small deeds of selflessness, look beyond self, dream of a better world. How tolerant and giving will our society be? Let us in our own small way help anyone we know who needs us by our side thus hoping that people may come forward and take it on from this by small gestures which may make a huge difference in the lives of many.

Listening to a friend, a child, or our elderly parents, calling people who need help, and to keep track of the sick and ailing doesn't require expertise or a big bank balance, it requires a particular temperament and that makes a huge difference to all who watch our actions which may in some way or the other motivate someone else to do the same. This does not require any theory, study, or any expert to tell us that good work and thoughts are contagious and should be replicated which is the need of the hour. To stay safe does not mean stay selfish, extend your helping hand because for all you know the next hand that requires help may be yours.